The Contemplative Way

Quietly Savoring God's Presence

Franz Jalics, SJ

TRANSLATED BY
Matthias Altrichter, SJ

Paulist Press
New York/Mahwah, NJ

43 - 54

Cover design by Sharyn Banks
Book design by Lynn Else

Copyright © 2011 by Franz Jalics, SJ .

English translation copyright © 2011 by Matthias Altrichter, SJ
Original Title: *Der Kontemplative Weg*, published in German
by Echter Verlag, Würzburg, Germany, 2006.
First English edition, The Bombay Saint Paul Society
ISBN 978-81-7109-859-0
Edited for publication in the United States by Ruth A. Fox, PhD

Library of Congress Cataloging-in-Publication Data

Jálics, Ferenc.
    [Kontemplative Weg. English]
    The contemplative way : quietly savoring God's presence / Franz
Jalics ; translated by Matthias Altrichter. — 1st English ed.
        p. cm.
    ISBN 978-0-8091-4722-9 (alk. paper)
    1. Contemplation. I. Title.
    BV5091.C7J3513 2011
    248.3'4—dc22

                                                    2011004466

Published by Paulist Press
997 Macarthur Boulevard
Mahwah, New Jersey 07430

www.paulistpress.com

Printed and bound in the
United States of America

Contents

Introduction

Contemplative moments come in our human lifetime when we get glimpses of something we have been waiting for all our lives. They may give us a little foretaste of a life that promises us more than our everyday routine experience. We are surprised by them and they leave behind a longing for deeper insights into life's secrets. We are given a glimpse of our true homeland.

It may happen to you out in the open, green pasture, or on top of a mountain—you suddenly experience a wide space around you that cannot be measured in miles. You are aware of something that has always been there but has never been noticed. While sitting at the lakeside, fishing—at an early morning hour, when the lake is still calm and the fish aren't yet biting—you are overwhelmed with an air of stillness. It is quite possible that you came to the lake not so much for fishing as for this moment of stillness.

A young woman I had introduced to contemplative prayer suddenly said, "Oh yes, I know that," and she went on to recall a swing in the garden out-

1

side her childhood home. Whenever she was over-come by a feeling of sadness or joy, she used to go out and sit quietly on that swing. There she would sit without doing anything. And there she would be filled with a life-giving stillness that would wipe away her sadness or multiply her joy. During her introduction to contemplative prayer, she remem-bered those moments of stillness again.

The sense of wonder, so typical of children, has a touch of contemplation. Others experience this touch in days of sickness or when smarting under the heavy burden of suffering. Perhaps they are not mature contemplatives, but they remember the touch. They realize that there is a dimension to life that cannot be affected by pain or weakness.

For others, a sudden brush with death may pro-vide a notion of this life-dimension. Still others experience something similar while engaged in humble and seemingly useless service to the poor and the mentally challenged. They claim that these people have really given them more than they themselves were able to give. In this "more" there is already a trace of contemplation. Many people find a growing serenity and equanimity in themselves, due only to the slow and steady process of matur-ing in and through their daily activities. This seren-ity helps them to conquer times of crisis. The contemplative foundation is forming inside them. Often one can see in their very eyes or in their radiance that they have learned to walk the way of contemplation.

Experiences of this kind may not yet be enough to bestow on you the contemplative way of life, which is the topic of this book. They will, however, entice you to continue walking toward contemplation and offer you a foretaste of it. Without these experiences, you would not be interested in the faith or the contemplative way.

In this book I want to present the meaning of the contemplative way simply, yet precisely. In the first chapters I try to clarify three concepts: faith, eternal life, and contemplation. Then I wish to offer concrete examples of the contemplative way. We will investigate its connections with philosophy, Sacred Scripture, and mysticism. We reflect upon contemplative prayer's development, its effect on our active life, and its relevance for our times. A final example will then show us what contemplative prayer is all about and how it may be translated into practical steps.

At the end of each chapter you will find questions designed not only to help you assimilate the content intellectually, but also to incorporate it into your life experiences.

1

The Path before Contemplation

Long before we reach the path to contemplation, most of us walk on the path of faith. We must never mistake the one for the other. Faith is the certainty of what I don't see and have not experienced (Heb 11:1). Contemplation, however, is not a certainty of the existence of God: it is an initial *vision* of God.

To believe in God means that I am sure God exists without my having seen him. This certainty is not based on a direct vision of God, but instead rests on three important experiences:

The first foundation of religious faith is life experience. Every human being harbors deep inside a notion of transcendence, a longing for God, and an intuition that there is life beyond death. Should it ever happen that I receive a definite message from God, this intuition will begin, as it were, to vibrate:

my faith is like a sounding board for such a message. The deeper and more intense my life experience, the easier the road to discovering my faith in God. I may also come to realize that the notion of God was present in me earlier, but because of the normal worries of daily life, I just had not paid enough attention to it. There is no faith without life experience. Therefore, the depth of your experience of life is a decisive factor in the formation of your faith in God.

Everybody will one day be confronted by the message of revelation. It is likely to come from church or another religious environment: from people (we may call them teachers, prophets, or masters) who proclaim the message, or from scriptures revealing an ancient tradition of wisdom about eternal life, or from a community embodying that wisdom. This is true of every religion, and it is the second decisive foundation of faith. When we experience teachers, scriptures, and community as authentic and credible, then we can build faith on them.

The third and most important foundation of faith is grace. God grants me the interior confirmation that I am walking in faith along the right path and that life beyond death is a reality rather than fiction or illusion. This conviction is necessary because faith in God implies that I define my life in alignment with God. God may lead a believer through the alternate paths of consolation and desolation, so that he or she may be able to recognize right decisions better and be confirmed in them.* Yes, light and darkness are part of my faith.

Faith in God is the certitude that our true origin is in God, that our earthly life is rooted in God, and that after this life on earth we will be taken up forever into a life of union with God's universal love in everlasting happiness. Faith, therefore, is not the experience of the vision of God, but it assures us of the certainty that this vision will be given to us. To remain true to the idea of this book, we will have to turn specifically to the promised life in God after death, as elaborated upon in the next chapter.

Dear Reader, as mentioned in the Introduction, I now wish to ask you questions. Please take time to answer them, for they are meant to help you approach the contemplative way through your own personal experience.

This chapter concludes with two: In what important experiences is your faith rooted? Of these, which are the most significant for you?

---

* The Spiritual Exercises of St. Ignatius [hereafter, Sp. Exer.]. 313f.

2

Our True Home

Deep down, human beings sense that this world and the life we now live are not the final word. We carry in us a longing that tells us, like a compass pointing ahead, that our earthly life with its sufferings and our death is merely a *way*—a return journey to God. In the depth of our souls we know that we too are spirit, and that we are only pilgrims in this universe, which is subject to limitations of space and time. Deep down, something tells us that our true home is God himself. It assures us that the God who planted us on this earth is really waiting for us, just as the father in the parable looked for his prodigal son (Luke 15:11–32).

All religions proclaim this good news. They have many names for it: transcendence, heaven, the "beyond," the kingdom of God, the kingdom of heaven, or eternal life. There we shall taste genuine bliss, free from pain and suffering.

Our Christian faith gives us the promise of something still much greater. It assures us that we shall see God face-to-face and "as he really is" (Matt 5:8; 1 John 3:2); that "God is love," and that we will be transformed into that love and will be given total union with him (John 17:11, 21).

These are almost unbelievable statements. God is a mystery, and the only way to speak about God is with deep reverence. Whatever we might think about God, one thing goes beyond all questioning: we will never be able to grasp God with our intellect. Our reasoning will never be able fully to comprehend him. Love alone, and quiet adoration, will help us touch him.

What revelation promises us here is truly inconceivable. If God, after our struggle in faith on earth and after our death, plans to lead us to the fulfillment of such promises, then his grace will have to bring about a mighty transformation in us. Only in faith are we sure of what we shall never be able to grasp by understanding, much less by sight or experience. God himself has to come and fill us with what he has promised. In this life, certainty will remain in the realm of hope, faith, and trust. Here and there, however, God is pleased even in this life, gently and secretly, to shower upon individuals (in the depth of their souls) this vision of himself. We call this the grace of contemplation. We will examine it more closely in the next chapter.

Dear Reader, does God remain for you—in spite of his closeness—an incomprehensible mystery, a mys-

tery that creates in you a feeling of reverent love and adoration?

When you find out that a person very dear and precious to you has just died, do only sadness and the thought of a cold tomb come to your mind? Or do you also think of the light and the life that are waiting for us?

3

What Is Contemplation?

The word *contemplation* means "the intuitive vision of the highest truths, and, in a religious sense, of God." In religious literature, synonyms for contemplation are *mystery* and *gazing*.*

Contemplation as the "vision of God" is pure grace (*contemplatio infusa*), because a human being cannot see God by his or her own efforts. This gift of God, however intense it may be, is different from the grace of faith, which, as we have seen in the first chapter, grants certainty of the existence of God,

---

* For this chapter I found helpful the definitions in the German *Lexikon für Theologie und Kirche*, 3rd ed. (Freiburg im Breisgau: Verlag Herder, 1997), and in the profound articles on contemplation and devotion in *Dictionnaire de Spiritualité*.

but not a vision of God. Faith does not cease with the first contemplative grace; however, an essential new element—the vision of God—lifts a person into a new state.

We must not mistake the grace of contemplation for that of *faith*, but it would be equally erroneous to mistake it for the grace of *consolation*. Consolation is an increase, a growth, in the certainty of faith (Sp. Exer., 316) but it is not a vision of God. This difference is also seen in the fact that the grace of contemplation may be experienced with or without consolation. *Devotion* (defined as surrender, spontaneity of love) is an equally significant grace and is important on our journey to God. It is not, however, a vision of God, but a pious feeling, a religious virtue. Neither must we identify the grace of contemplation with "looking at" (*contemplari* in Latin) or meditating on religious objects, such as pictures and icons, or meditating on inspiring thoughts, texts, or events. The grace of contemplation is a vision (also *contemplari*) of God himself, even though often as if through a veil. We should be equally careful not to identify the grace of contemplation with the complete vision of God in eternal life, the *visio beatifica*.

The grace of contemplation, then, raises a person to a state between faith and eternal life. It leads beyond faith because it gives, not only certainty, but a real vision of God. It does not, however, grant the full vision of God in everlasting life: "Now we see in a mirror, dimly, but then we will see face to face" (1 Cor 13:12).

The grace of contemplation shows an immediate *effect*: it quickens an irresistible passion to reach ever more deeply into this vision of God. The person whom God has once granted an initial and fleeting glance of his essence is fascinated to such a degree that, from then on, he or she is occupied only with one desire: to see God. Such a person longs to direct his or her gaze on God alone and so to rest at God's feet. "When shall I come and behold the face of God?" cries the psalmist (Ps 42:2). The Old Testament dedicates a whole book to this hunger for God: the Song of Songs.

Such a passion is the clearest way to identify those who are ready for the contemplative way. Others, however, who have never tasted that grace or felt this hunger, will not be able to appreciate the inner passion for contemplation. They will be tempted to think that those seeking the contemplative way are merely preoccupied with sterile methods of prayer. Still others may feel that contemplatives are escaping the world, in spite of the fact that these very people, with the exception perhaps of a few hermits, are more engaged in the service of others than the rest of humankind.

Contemplative prayer is the *answer* to the grace of contemplation, just as faith is the response to proclamation; and the opening of a flower, the result of the sun's rays and rain. The grace of contemplation creates in us a passion for God, a desire to see God face-to-face. This passion expects a reply. And the response is this: the person will direct her or his gaze more and more immediately to the vision of Jesus Christ or God the Father. This prayerful response is what we may call *contemplative prayer*. Such prayer is an attempt to orient all mental activities, all preoccupation with emotions and religious imagery or with plans for the future, toward the vision of God. In Christianity the best known and the most frequently practiced kind of contemplative prayer is the Jesus Prayer.

This is the sense of contemplative exercises, or a retreat, about which I am speaking. Neither contemplative prayer nor contemplative retreats presuppose the actual presence of contemplative grace. Prayer and retreats aim at but one thing: to prepare ourselves for this grace, to be ready for it—to dispose ourselves, as it were (Sp. Exer., 1:3), independent of whether infused grace was granted by God or not. Obviously, God may work in our hearts long before we think of disposing ourselves for grace; however, the work of appropriately disposing ourselves is the one and only thing we can do to prepare the ground for the grace of contemplation. We will come back to this topic later.

The passion to see God himself will not remain hidden in the depths of our souls. Besides permeating our prayer life, it will permeate and transform our relationship with the world around us. We shall also return to both these aspects later.

A word about terminology: *meditation* in the Christian sense is a kind of prayer in which we go to God with the help of texts, pictures, and thoughts; we adore God, we address God, we make petitions to God, and we make resolutions for the future before God. In the course of the twentieth century, however, in the context of what are called "Eastern practices," the term *meditation* came to be understood in the contemplative sense. This may lead, of course, to misunderstandings, but we shall not pay more attention to them now. On the other hand, Ignatius calls his reflections on the life of Jesus *contemplacions*, yet his description shows that they are not contemplations in the sense we use the word here, but meditations in the original Christian sense.

❧

Dear Reader, are there times when you pray, when you talk with God about your life, that you make petitions or promises, you express repentance, or you plan something in God's presence?

Then again, at other times, are you are so fascinated with God that your only desire is to be lost in the silence of God's presence, without a word or even a thought? If you have said yes to both questions, do you observe differences between the two experiences?

4

Testimony

In the first three chapters we have tried to define the basic concepts of the contemplative way. Now let us listen to an account that takes the form of personal testimony in order to represent that way descriptively. My aim is, on the one hand, to give a concrete idea of the contemplative experience and, on the other, to incorporate it into the context of Christian living.

I was always a Christian, in spite of the fact that my life did not move along smoothly in ways the church would expect. I felt at home in this world. I did not pay much attention to the Ten Commandments, and the only meaning I saw in life was to enjoy it. I did not know, and wasn't much interested in, what comes after death. On the rare occasions when I did sit down to pray, my personal interests were at the forefront. I only realized much later that, while I was in this state, Ignatius would have made me undergo the First Week of the Spiritual Exercises. (We will return to this in chapter 13.)

Later, I was granted the grace of a conversion. I discovered Jesus Christ, or rather, he entered my life. His life became my home. The goal of my life now was Jesus Christ and no longer the material world. My prayer was to go more deeply into the life of Jesus, who had become my Master and Lord, and I followed him. In my meditation on his life, I became aware of my deep-rooted problems and inclinations, and I mustered enough courage to rid myself of them.

Turning to Jesus—seeing his life as exemplary— I began to discover my tasks in the world. I began to live for him alone, and I tried to find him in every situation of my life. I renounced the world, yet, in fact, renouncing it had a new meaning for me: Jesus Christ, I felt, was calling me to change the world, so that it might completely become his kingdom, his mystical body. Out of my love for Jesus, I invested my whole self and committed all my faculties to the sanctification of the world. I wanted to liberate myself from all that fettered me to this world, so as to live for Christ in poverty and to incarnate his kingdom on earth. My prayer, my search, my daily decisions, and my work were done in service to Jesus Christ. I knew that I could not bring it about by my own efforts, but with his help and in the community of the church, I labored toward this goal. Years later, I realized that Ignatius, in the meditations on the life of Jesus, aimed at this surrender and this readiness to serve. His Spiritual Exercises focus on this part of the way, from the Second and Third Week up to Christ's ascension, meditated on in the Fourth Week.

I saw a subtle change in myself. I sensed it as the beginning of a contemplative way. I noticed this new orientation first in my prayer life, whereas my work and my service for Christ in the world remained as they were before; at least I did not observe any change.

It all began with a grace that stirred up in me a passionate love and longing to see the face of God. I sensed an irresistible pull to be still and to remain lost in the silent presence of the Risen Christ. Gazing at him and just resting in his presence absorbed all my attention. This silent presence and the repetition of the name *Jesus Christ* filled my prayer life. It was not just a "prayer method," as some others seemed to feel, but a fundamental necessity welling up from within. I wanted only to let myself be irradiated by him and for him to stream through me. I did not exclude other ways of praying, such as personal conversation with God, but the repetition of Jesus' name became the center of gravity in my prayer.

I opened the Gospels, but my meditations on the life of Jesus and my reflections on how to change myself became, at first, more and more simple; they finally vanished altogether. I could neither reflect nor engage in discernment. To meditate on pictures seemed to me a mere waste of time compared to the direct gaze on the Risen Lord's presence. I did not want to be concerned any longer with questions of how to change myself or what I should do for Christ. Thus I moved from thinking and discerning and other ways of prayer to looking at, paying attention to, and resting in the presence of God, and to focusing on his name. That silent prayer brought about relentless confrontations with my inordinate inclinations (fear, insecurity, troubling thoughts, and so forth). I now found it much tougher to escape from them than my earlier ways of meditating had allowed. Why? Because, in this gazing at the presence of Christ, I had come closer to the deepest center of my being.

"Our hearts are restless until they find our rest in You," said Augustine. I had heard this and similar texts many times before. It was only now that I began truly to *experience* them; and this was because I would now spend many hours, intently alert, without words, without thoughts, and without images, in simple gazing at God.

When I mentioned this to some of my friends and even to my spiritual guide, they appeared worried, fearing that I might become estranged from life. What happened, however, was the exact opposite.

My worrying over how to change the world was now no longer part of my prayer. If I met with success, I knew immediately that the achievement was not mine. It had only happened through me. That brought about an unbelievable sense of freedom in me, because I did not need to achieve anything. Now I know what grace is. My deep experience is that I myself do nothing: it is he who is working through me. When I realized this, I remembered the Sermon on the Mount: the birds of the air, the lilies of the field—have no worry, all will be given to you (Matt 6:25). Those prophets came to mind who had made it their aim, not so much to preach, as to announce what God urged them to say. St. Paul says, "The love of Christ urges us on" (2 Cor 5:14).

These developments in my prayer experience have had marvelous effects on my life in the world. Each time I return from the hour of stillness to my daily activities, I do so as a new man. The stillness has filled me with clarity, strength, and joy. Out of that center of my life, I see the world around me differently. I find an increasing flow of love to all people. I also tolerate troublesome situations more easily. All it takes is for me to return, for a brief moment, to the core of my being, and the stress and heaviness of life become relative: they lose their power over me.

I think of Ignatius, who said that it would take him just a quarter of an hour to accept the liquidation of the Society of Jesus—the greatest achievement of his life—with inner calm. That is exactly my experience today. Strength and clarity for my life do not come anymore from my reflections and decisions: they emanate effortlessly from my deeper self.

Before I had made this discovery about the contemplative way, I often heard people say that, by spending time in prayer, we lose precious time that could have been used for some gainful activity—that prayer really makes you unfit for life in the world. Now from experience I know that I work more than ever, because I feel more energy coming from within, and because I manage to live without stress. I now begin to understand Jesus, who, after a day of intense activity—conversations, healings, contact with people—withdrew for prayer for several hours of the night. In doing so he returned to the core of his being, there to come face-to-face with his Father, to be filled with new energy.

The effectiveness of all I do doesn't come any longer from my organizing, my "making it happen," but it comes from the radiance. In the past I endeavored to go out to people to bring Christ to them. Since I turned within, however, I find that more and more people are coming to me, and they, too, seem to notice that there is more power in what I say. I have seen the same results in other people who have learned to live out of an inner stillness. Their effectiveness radiates. I think of Jesus Christ himself, of whom Mark says that "power had gone forth from him" (Mark 5:30) and healed people. I am reminded that Moses climbed down from Mount Sinai with radiance on his face (Exod 34:29–35), and that St. Paul says he preached in the power of the Spirit (1 Cor 2:4). Of course, I am far from having the kind of radiance whose brilliance was at work in them. Yet I begin to sense that my influence on others is no longer my own doing, but that it all comes from the Spirit of God, who is flowing through me.

I find a difference even in making decisions now: instead of laboring at length over the process of deciding, I try to be lost in deep inner stillness, and from that deeper center, to this day, new clarity has always surfaced. Again Jesus comes to mind, who, according to the Gospel of John, only had to turn to the Father within and then knew what he had to say. I think of Ignatius and his first "time" for making a decision (Sp. Exer., 175). One's choice is manifested with inner clarity and without any human effort. Ignatius mentions as a good example the way that the apostle Matthew followed the Lord without hesitation.

We no longer need to make resolutions in our prayers or at the end of a retreat. The guarantee of progress is now no longer a matter of our willing acts, as it was formerly. Our progress and growth will be in proportion to the intensity and duration of the time we have rested in God's presence. We don't attempt, as formerly, to change the world; the changes come about without our planning. That gives us great freedom. If ever I still need to make a resolution, it is only this one: to persevere along the way, in the prayer of stillness. There is nothing else I have to achieve. If in the past I have struggled to change the world for Christ, now I only sit back and observe how the Lord is doing all of it, using me as his tool.

My contact with people is now on a deeper level. I have discovered that the depth of one's relationship with others depends on the depth you have reached in your own self first. Through gazing on God, I have become much more united in my self on deeper levels, and consequently also united with other human beings. Prolonged stillness has steadily refined my intuitive understanding of others. Of course, that is bound to improve your communication with people because your empathy has now also reached new levels.

In sum, the contemplative way has changed my relationship with God as well as with the world. My relationship with God has now turned from thinking and doing to simple looking or gazing, not of course on the complete vision of God—rather, a steady gazing at his presence.

My relationship with the world is also now different. I no longer see the world as the way to God. The world is not the way to God, but the Way leads me from God to the world. It is not where I want to exercise my service for Christ, but I am in the world, and God is changing the world through me. I don't live in the world in order to come to God, but—because I am coming from God—I am now able to radiate love in the world. I am merely a tool in God's hands. God is doing it all, and I allow myself to be used. I may have sensed this earlier, but now it is my reality.

Dear Reader, can you imagine that, in the midst of doubts and problems, simply staying with and turn-

ing toward Jesus will bring about clarity and give you a new dynamic in all your external activities?

5

Five Minutes
of Philosophy

The Gospel of John tells of an interesting encounter between Jesus and a Samaritan woman. Jesus asks her to give him water to drink. The woman, impressed by Jesus' extraordinary perceptiveness, asks about the place where God is to be worshiped.

"Sir, I see that you are a prophet. Our ancestors worshiped on this mountain, but you say that the place where people must worship is in Jerusalem." Jesus said to her, "Woman, believe me, the hour is coming when you will worship the Father neither on this mountain nor in Jerusalem....The hour is coming, and is now here, when the true worshipers will worship the Father in spirit and truth, for the Father seeks such as these to worship him" (John 4:19–21, 23). Jesus' answer is clear. Adoration of the Father is not tied to some space. It has to be done on the level of the Spirit. The Father is Spirit and is to be adored in the Spirit. What is Jesus intending to say? We are always tied to the body and thus tied to space. Somewhere in us, are we mere spirit? Where in the temple of our body is that sanctuary, that center, where we are only spirit? Where in us is the divine light that, like God, is pure spirit?

These questions have been asked by all great philosophers. Actually, they form the central problem of philosophy. That is why I dare, dear reader, to pull you for a moment into the world of philosophy. Human beings are body and spirit. Everything we do or think always has a spiritual and a bodily pole. For example, our thoughts: On the one hand they are spirit, and on the other hand they have a bodily dimension, because they are also the result of the brain's activity, and the brain is body. Without the brain there is no thinking. God does not think, he knows. Scholastic philosophy claims that angels, too, lack the capacity to think. They have intuition, but cannot think. They have no brain.

Do we possess, somewhere inside of us, a place, a center, or a base where we are only spirit, to which our body has no access? Many philosophers have actually found that place. Let us take one example each from several time frames: ancient, medieval, and modern.

"I know that I don't know," said Socrates. "I know" here means "I am conscious of"—but conscious of what? Socrates wants to say that by looking deep into himself he is reaching a state of consciousness where there is nothing left except his existence. I know that I am. Beyond that my consciousness is blank. What remains is that I know that I don't know anything. That would be a glimpse of the pure spirit. When I am wide awake and, at the same time, my consciousness is empty, then I am in my center. There we are only spirit—and nearest to God, who is pure Spirit. It is simple consciousness: a conscious *being there*. In that place a human being is the "image of God" to the highest degree. There he or she may get a glimpse of what it means to be one with God. As long as we linger there, we remain in pure adoration. That is adoration in the spirit.

The medieval Scholastics approached this question from a different point of view. They stated that nothing in our consciousness can be pure spirit. Why? Because everything that enters consciousness enters through our senses. But whatever passed through the senses will always be related to the body and, therefore, is not pure spirit. In Latin: *Nihil est in intellectu quod non prius fuerit in sensu* ("There is nothing in our consciousness unless it passed through the senses first"). However, the Scholastics added an exception: *nisi ipse intellectus* ("except the intellect itself"). The exception is the light of consciousness itself that never passed through the senses. It is pure spirit. If the light of consciousness is aware of itself, it is pure spirit. Only there are we, in the full sense, "his image and likeness." To stay and remain in this pure spirit—that is adoration in the spirit.

Martin Heidegger, a leading German philosopher of the twentieth century, speaks of the "*soseinsfreien Daseinserkenntnis*." *Daseinserkenntnis* could be translated "awareness of existence"; that is, to be conscious of the fact that one exists. *Sosein* expresses the nature of being: its limitations and characteristics. The word *soseinsfrei* means the absence of any characteristic or limitation that makes a thing this or that way. There is nothing tangible in my consciousness, no limited thing, no form, no "being a certain way." The pure awareness of existence is pure spirit. There true adoration is bound to take place.

If there is something definitely absolute, then everything else will be made relative in relation to it. Such is that spiritual point found by the philosophers, an absolutely immovable point: a true center. If I rest in it, then everything else will become relative, and all will fall into place around this absolute point, this center. In it, only a thin film of curtain separates us from the presence of God. Through the experience of this pure spirit, everything is bound to find its place from within, without our having to think about it. The great experiences of a call that Ignatius mentions in the first election time (Sp. Exer., 175), are they not of this kind? Contemplative prayer is about this: we direct our attention toward that focal point and rise by grace to its source. To persevere there is the highest level of adoration, not through words, not through actions, but much deeper: through *being*.

☙

Dear Reader, I have described the spiritual core of a person as understood by three philosophical schools. Have you ever experienced this very center of yours? Have you had the experience of being simply there, and have you felt completely one with yourself?

<hr>

6

The Two Stages of Poverty

Nowhere has Jesus put the foundation for contemplation as clearly and comprehensibly as in the dialogue with the rich young man (Mark 10:17–31). This young person asks how to achieve eternal life. To this Jesus has two answers, which are like two stages of spiritual life. The first consists in keeping the Ten Commandments, the second in following Jesus personally. Jesus sees where this man stands in spiritual life and suggests to him: "Keep the commandments"; that is, keep to everything necessary for gaining eternal life. The man replies that he has walked on the suggested way for a long time but has exhausted its possibilities, and he asks whether there might not be something to lead him still further. Jesus turns to him and offers him the way of following Jesus. He tells him to sell everything he has and then to walk the way that Jesus himself walks: "Go, sell what you have…and follow me." The man would have to give up all his possessions, something he is not prepared to do at that time. His home is still on this earth. Heaviness and sadness come over him and he walks away.

The disciples are shocked by Jesus' suggestion. If we have to let go of everything, they say, who can be saved? Instead of pacifying the disciples, Jesus reinforces their apprehensions: Yes, it is impossible! At least, for human beings it is unachievable. You cannot walk that path. Then he says that there is nothing impossible for God. This contrast of the powerlessness of humanity with the omnipotence of God shows the meaning of poverty: a person has to become empty to be filled by God. Yet this poverty is not negative or destructive because it leads to the fullness of God.

But for Jesus even this is not enough. He continues the conversation and confirms once again the radicalism of such emptiness. "A camel will sooner go through the eye of a needle than a rich man enter the kingdom of God." The "eye of a needle" is a small narrow gate, as the entrance to a courtyard was once called. A camel's load used to hang on both sides of the animal. Unless first freed from that load, it could not enter the courtyard. Jesus wanted to say that discipleship is like passing through that narrow gate: impossible as long as you are heavily burdened. You have to get rid of everything, to be completely empty.

This teaching of the two ways is not a casual episode in the Gospel. It permeates all of Jesus' message. He speaks alternately from the perspective of one way or the other. Some teachings are clearly meant for those walking in the way of the Ten Commandments. When Jesus says that one should not kill, not swear an oath, not commit adultery (Matt 5:21–38), he refers to such people. The Beatitudes, on the other hand, refer to the way of discipleship: "Blessed are the poor in spirit" (Matt 5:3). We should be attentive when reading the Gospels to understand when Jesus speaks to people who find themselves at one or the other stage of belief.

The important question we have to ask now is this: does Jesus speak only of material possessions, or does he have in mind also mental, psychic, and spiritual treasures?

Do I also have to let go of human deeds, thoughts, memories, preoccupation with feelings, consolation, plans, discernment, decisions, resolutions, and all kinds of activities? He mentions explicitly only treasures that I can sell and for which I receive payment. The point here, however, is that I receive treasures in heaven in return. Things I don't let go of remain "treasures on earth" and do not become "treasures in heaven." In other words, we have to become empty so that we may be filled with God. All that I do not let go of will remain merely treasures of this world and will never be treasures of heaven. God, however, also wants to fill our psychic and mental activities. Yes, it is also very much a matter of our psychic and spiritual treasures. They cannot be excluded from the grace of contemplation. Jesus demands self-emptying to the level of a simple existence. The Letter to the Philippians shows us the way of emptiness in the life of Jesus Christ himself. Jesus walked the way of radical self-emptying:

> Have among yourselves the same attitude that is also yours in Christ Jesus,

>> Who, though he was in the form of God,
>>> did not regard equality with God
>>>> something to be grasped.
>> Rather, he emptied himself,
>>> taking the form of a slave,
>>> coming in human likeness;
>> and found human in appearance,
>>> he humbled himself,
>>> becoming obedient to death,
>>> even death on a cross.
>>>>>> (Phil 2:5–8, NAB)

The self-emptying of Jesus is complete: even to death on the cross. He also surrendered his thoughts, imaginations, and feelings. All who wish to walk along that steep path are called to do precisely that. We, too, have to become empty—not to remain empty, but to be filled with God.

The mystery of the death and resurrection of Jesus extends to all Christians. It is the central message of Christianity, a message we celebrate on Easter: "If any want to become my followers, let them deny themselves and take up their cross and follow me" (Mark 8:34). "Unless a grain of wheat falls into the earth and dies, it remains just a single grain; but if it dies, it bears much fruit" (John 12:24). "Those who want to save their life will lose it" (Matt 16:25). Thus, the invitation to be empty also extends to our mental, psychic, and spiritual activities.

Reflections on death have always been of great importance in Christian spirituality. Many Christians once placed a skull on their table to be reminded of death. There were monks who used to greet each other, *"Memento mori"* ("Remember that you will die"). Those who accompany the dying as the final hour approaches could share a lot about the need to be empty. Individuals have gone through a so-called borderline or near-death experience. For them it was like passing through a door to catch a glimpse of "the beyond," an experience of total fulfillment in total emptiness.

Thus, we can say that the invitation to sell everything comprises two stages. The first is the selling of all material possessions. The second stage implies the renunciation of all spiritual treasures; that is, thinking, all psychic activities, the will, and everything we want to make or do as humans. Only then will we be truly poor. Only then will we have died to the world to live in God.

If we now apply all this to prayer, we will have to say that all images, thoughts, consolations, considerations, discernments, decisions, resolutions, and occupation with feelings and emotions—all these surely belong to a committed faith as part of our discipleship, but not to the contemplative way. All these focus on change of self, on the outer world, and on our relationship to God. They are still "doing," a spiritual doing, but still a "doing." They are an asset to our prayer. It may be a "doing" for Jesus, but it still remains a "doing." That is why we have to say that reflections, meditations, and the "application of senses" belong to our practice of faith, but not to the contemplative way, not to simple contemplative looking or gazing

How would a prayer of this kind—of radical emptiness and contemplative surrender—how would that sound? Let us take an example:

Take, Lord, and receive all my liberty, my memory, my understanding, and all my will— all that I have and possess. You, Lord, have

given all that to me. I now give it back to
you, O Lord. All of it is yours. Dispose of it
according to your will. Give me your love
and your grace, for that is enough for me.
(Sp. Exer., 234)

❧

*Dear Reader, how do you feel about this prayer? Can
you make it all your own? Where do you feel resistance, and where does it awaken in you a desire for
the contemplative way?*

7

The Private Room
and the Balcony

Jesus speaks explicitly about this poverty (renunciation of all spiritual treasures) in prayer itself.
"Whenever you pray, go into your room and
shut the door and pray to your Father who is in
secret; and your Father who sees in secret will
reward you" (Matt 6:6). The "room" here means a
storeroom or treasury without windows. Once the
door is shut, no one can look out or in. There you

are hidden. There is only one thing your eyes may turn to, according to the text: the Father.

As long as someone is preoccupied in prayer with thoughts, feelings, emotions, or images, he is not yet in his private room. Maybe he is already in the house, but sitting on the balcony. He relishes the marvelous sight of his surroundings; that is, the world outside. His thoughts and observations, his planning and his discerning, all are still connected with the world out there. He can happily occupy himself with his own psycho-religious landscape, for thoughts and feelings connect us with the world and with our psyche.

According to Jesus, this is not yet your "private room," not yet a lightless abode. The door is not bolted yet. You are not yet in the darkness of that room. Your true change is not yet accomplished; you have not yet passed through the "eye of the needle." The final passage to the interior lies between the balcony and the private room, where the Father alone sees us, where no thoughts and no feelings will bother us anymore. Only the empty, questionless center, the dark private room, exists.

However, you are not to suppress your feelings here. All feelings may come and go; otherwise we are blocked. But in that private room, the empty center, the basis of your being, there are no feelings—only plain awareness. God himself is at the deepest center. He abides at the foundation of our being. That is why we have to leave the balcony and enter farther into the private room. Our gaze there is focused completely on the Father. Only the person who can abide in this center will have the freedom in the outside world that Ignatius calls "indifference": "not to seek...a long life rather than a short one," and to remain unperturbed in the face of what fate has in store (Sp. Exer., 23:6–7). It is not enough to renounce those desires through willpower. We may resist *fulfilling* the desires through willpower, but we cannot uproot the desires themselves. Clearly we don't have the power not to sense them. But they will be burnt up by our looking, our turning to the presence of God.

The Gospel of Mark gives us a clear example of radical emptiness, the absence of thoughts: "When they bring you to trial and hand you over, do not worry beforehand about what you are to say; but say whatever is given you at that time, for it is not you who speak, but the Holy Spirit" (Mark 13:11). The accused should become completely empty. He should not seek security in his eloquence, nor in his evidence, nor in his lawyers. The Holy Spirit will speak through him from within. As long as he relies on lawyers or reflects on the arguments with which he might defend himself, it is only he himself speaking, and not the Holy Spirit. Mark's example is a matter of the second level of poverty that Jesus demands of us.

❧

Dear Reader, where do you go when you wish to pray? Do you remain on your balcony, or do you withdraw to your private room in order to rest there under the gaze of the Father? Or have you experienced something like this: in preparing for a difficult conversation or a threatening encounter, have you spent time sitting in stillness, trusting that the right words will be given from within, at the right time?

8

Immediacy

Human beings need a medium, a means, of getting in touch with one another. If I wish to contact a friend far away, I write him a letter. If he replies, we are in touch through correspondence. If, however, he turns up personally, I stop reading his letters. Our letters have done their job. Now we put them aside so that they don't interfere with our communication. Instead of reading letters, we begin to talk to each other. We have chosen a new means, conversation, that unites us more deeply than did the letters. If sharing makes us feel closer and closer, we may find that even words are too much of an interference, no longer needed. What remains is eye contact, also a means of communication; we just look at each other. At a certain moment even this may be too much: the quiet feeling of being together is enough. Our hearts expand, and we sense that we have come closer than before, when those mediators of words and looks stood between us.

The aim of the different means is to bring about encounter. They only have a transitory function. Necessary at first, then helpful, later superfluous, they may even begin to interfere. Finally, they might actually obstruct deeper encounters.

Jesus took that way with his disciples. They came to know him in Galilee. He made use of all human means to bring them together with himself, from language to a life in common. By his death, the disciples were deprived of these intermediaries, and during his appearances after the resurrection, talking and eating together played only a supplementary role. Jesus touched his disciples in a more immediate way. Soon he ascended into heaven, depriving them of his presence, but returned as the Spirit, flooding them and guiding them from within; they call him the "Spirit of Jesus" (Acts 16:7). The only mediator now, if we can even call it that, is listening within.

This can tell us a lot about our journey to God: Faith needs to be communicated. Faith is lived in community—through the word of the Gospel, in the church, through books, through the events of life, and through the works of mercy. Faith grows in prayer, with the help of religious images, through insights that help us to progress, through considerations and meditations. All these are necessary on our path of faith. They are all helpful in bringing us closer to Jesus Christ and God the Father. However, God meets us with his grace, and then the means become more and more permeable, opening up until encounter becomes immediate.

This process of moving from the exterior to the interior is clearly seen in the Eucharist. First we celebrate the Liturgy of the Word. The words, the images, Holy Scripture, and the homily transmit closeness with God. Then we have the intercessions, often expressing personal and particular needs. This is fitting here. In the prayer over the offering we renew our surrender to God. Then, through the consecration, the body and blood of Jesus become present. Stillness spreads within. Through communion we receive Jesus' body and blood, and so he comes still closer, directly into our hearts through his body and blood. Then comes a precious period of quiet, with as few words as possible—words expressing the union between humanity and God, as "you in me and I in you" or "you are everything, I am nothing."

Lingering on in that stillness now means surrender, service of God, and adoration. Is there still a place for any medium? Everyone senses that talk after communion would be out of place. Encounter with Christ at this moment is of greater immediacy than spoken words. The Mass is teaching us in a concrete way to move from external means of encounter to immediacy. I am not saying that we should no longer recite prayers after communion or read. But we are invited to shift the weight of our devotion from words to mere stillness. Once deeply touched, an individual will want to do just that. It is an invitation. Everyone will do whatever corresponds to his or her actual state of development.

Something similar happens in prayer itself. John Marie Vianney, the holy parish priest from Ars, related how he saw a simple farmer in his church who spent long hours before the altar lost in prayer, without a book in his hands. When the priest once asked the farmer what he was doing while kneeling for so long, his answer was simple: "I look at him and he looks at me." Clearly, for this man, the means had been simplified to mere looking. Imagine a spiritual director turning up and telling him, "No, no, dear man, you must not be inactive or lazy like that, you have to take up Sacred Scripture and labor over a text. Only then may you look again on Christ." Would this not be placing obstacles between God and the individual, creating an impediment? Once the means had been reduced for this farmer to a simple gazing, we would only confuse him with tools he doesn't need anymore. He already has the message of Sacred Scripture internalized: it is now alive in his heart.

Images, thoughts, and feelings will always remain means in an encounter. Only awareness will make immediacy possible. Therefore, it is imperative to advance from thoughts and pictures to awareness and to looking or "gazing."

You can adore God with words, of course. And adoration may be embodied in actions, in which a person honors God through God's creation. However, there is also adoration through being: simply to exist for God. This is the deepest adoration because of its immediacy. When we persevere on the way of immediacy, we may come closer and closer to a state of oneness with Christ.

Ignatius must have taken great care with the people he trained as retreat directors. He was a man of few words, and still in his Exercises he returns twice to warn of a possible mistake. He knew that the promise to be "one with God" is given to us. He must have observed that some of his trainees seriously obstructed this way of immediacy in those they were supposed to guide. They tended unknowingly to place themselves between their retreatants and God through their talks, texts, and counsels. Therefore, he demanded that they respect the immediate encounter of the retreatant with God (Sp. Exer., 15:6 and 2:2–4).

⌘

Dear Reader, do you remember experiences in your life of interpersonal encounters in which you have reached great immediacy, either step by step or suddenly?

9

To Look Within

How can we dispose ourselves for the grace of contemplation? Everything we have done in our life until now—for God, for our neighbor, or for ourselves—will dispose us, at least remotely, for that grace. Imitation of Christ in poverty, the service of others, and all our life of prayer have always led us in the direction of contemplation and eternal life, if only indirectly. But a direct and immediate preparation for this grace does exist.

For eternal life we have two sure promises: We will be one with God (John 17:20–26), and we will see God as he is (1 John 3:2). The question therefore is: How can we prepare ourselves for this oneness with God and for the vision of God? What kinds of steps could make us dispose ourselves for and become receptive to it?

First, we consider *oneness with God*. This promise is not about some future point in time, for that would imply that one day we would become some kind of addition to God, which would cause a change in the nature of God. God, however, cannot change. He does not exist in time. If ever we will be one with God, we must now already be one with him, and only then will we become fully conscious of this oneness. The change takes place only in our consciousness. We may ask ourselves whether even now we already know something about this oneness with God. Revelation is a help in our search for answers.

Just imagine that we are standing in front of a mighty tree with huge branches. If I asked one of the branches, "Are you branch or are you tree?" it would have to answer, "I am branch and I am tree and I am one." If I went on asking, "What makes you think that you are tree?" it would have to answer that it knows this through the life energy that passes through it, because it is at the same time the life energy of the tree as well as of the branch. Consequently it will know this also through its fruits, since the fruits growing on it will be fruits of the tree rather than its own. I could then tell the branch, "Look closely at the force flowing through you and then follow it up to the very source, where the force is no longer branch, but tree. That is how it will dawn on you, that you are all one with the tree."

Jesus makes this comparison in the Gospel of John. "I am the vine, you are the branches" (John 15:1). Our fruits are altogether his. Without him we can never bear fruit. Once we understand that we do nothing and that he does everything through us, we have the "oneness" experience. We only have to look at the life force that produces fruits in us, and to follow it up to its very source. This way we will experience how we are one with him.

But the vine is, of course, not the only image in the Bible leading us to the source. Paul frequently says that we are members of Christ. If I am the hand of Christ, I am equally one with him, just as the branches are with the vine. Paul's description of our oneness with Christ is remarkable: he says, "It is no longer I who live, but it is Christ who lives in me" (Gal 2:20). In this case, too, Paul only has to look inside himself in order to see Christ. Paul says further that we are temples of the Holy Spirit. All we need to do is to look inside in order to discover the tabernacle of the Spirit. The Gospel explains this in a simple way: "The kingdom of God is within you" (Luke 17:21, KJV). When Jesus says that he is the life (John 11:25; 14:6), we only have to look once more inside to see directly the life in us. In order to dispose ourselves for the grace of contemplation, we have to look deeper and deeper inside, until we discover in our core how we are one with God.

We asked ourselves how to dispose ourselves for this oneness with God. The answer we have found till now is that we have to turn within intensively, to become aware of the life energy in us, and to follow it to its source. In the silent core, the ground of our being, is hidden the mystery of our oneness with Christ.

Next, we consider the *vision of God*. How can we prepare ourselves for it? Dear Reader, you have surely already noticed something interesting. Since we began to speak of a serious turning within, the verb we had to use for it was always "looking." At the most we can substitute synonyms like "being aware," "being conscious," "paying attention to," or "being there"—because at that depth, there are no thoughts, no images, no kinds of considerations, no "*making* it happen." Everything happens only through looking (gazing) and being. And with that we come to the second promise of eternal life: we shall see God.

In order to dispose ourselves for that vision, we have to learn a way of praying that consists more and more in looking; that is, we have to learn to change our praying into looking. In the depth where we are searching for immediate contact with God, there is nothing but looking and being. Everything else can only be a remote preparation. To dispose yourself immediately for the grace of contemplation means to say good-bye to thinking and doing and to persevere in looking at the center.

This effort will require constant discipline, because thinking and making will always connect us with the outer world. The changeover begins with looking at and listening to what is lying there in front of us: a flower, the blue sky, or the wide open space. It is all a matter of awareness. Seeing, hearing, touching, tasting, and smelling are all perceptions of the senses. The perception itself is mental in nature, because we perceive with our mind. But what we perceive comes through our senses.

Because of this, we say we are dealing with sensory perceptions. It is these that we begin with, until we learn to turn our attention more and more within, to life in us, to our consciousness, to the presence and the Now: to Being. We need to learn to remain in this looking.

Whether it is we ourselves who strive to prepare for the grace of contemplation, or God who surprises us with that grace before we discover it, it is always grace that pulls us in with elemental force in prayer. By whatever road we may reach contemplative prayer, it always comes with a growing desire to discover God within. Whether a hermit or a business executive, suddenly someone will find time for prayer, to encounter stillness within oneself.

If we remain looking, a power will bubble forth from our center and provide us with a marvelous blossoming of all our activities. It is the power of the vine, permeating our life and adding fruit a hundredfold to our activities. Preparing yourself for the grace of contemplation comprises a twofold change: from the outer world to the world within, and from thinking and doing to looking.

It may be helpful to remark here that there could be a danger of mistaking contemplation for religious feeling or consolation. Contemplation does not have much in common with feelings and devotion. It happens rather on the level of spiritual awareness or being. A contemplative experience will admittedly often bring feelings with it, but it may also come without any feelings. All churchgoers of goodwill have religious feelings and sense consolation. Consolation comes from God. God wants to orient our decision making by way of consolation and desolation; however, they belong to the area of faith and emotional life, but not to that of looking (Sp. Exer., 316, 4). Thus, they are not contemplative graces yet. There is a vital difference between feeling and spiritual looking. A contemplative person desires to look at God, independent of the fact whether she or he has feelings or not. That is why images, thoughts, and consolations are not helpful to the person. Rather than feeling consolation and devotion, all one longs for is to persevere in one's center, with one's view to God, even though feelings are absent.

❧

Dear Reader, do you remember some moments in your life when you abided in intense wonder? During such moments you were free of thoughts, without doing anything, and you were completely within yourself. Allow yourself to envision how such wonder could open up for you a new way to God!

10

Stillness

When two people are silent together, a soothing stillness where love flows can connect them. There could also be an embarrassing kind of stillness, however, full of tension and blockades, a stillness before a storm, or a silence without hope of communication. Most of the time when two people sit together in silence, they have to say something to each other. If they have been able to express everything, so that their messages really reached each other, love flows and pleasant stillness ensues. But when they have not been able to express themselves, communication is blocked, and they are walled off from each other. This stillness is unbearable. It makes no difference why they cannot tell each other what they have to say. They may be impeded because they themselves do not know what to say, or perhaps because they know that the other cannot receive and accept their message. They are not likely to tolerate this silence for long. It is the silence of the grave, and their messages will remain buried.

In our silence before God, something quite similar might happen. As long as our message is not expressed to him, that silence may be strained. As soon as we have poured out all our misery to God, the stillness becomes pleasant. If the communication is blocked, however, it may be because you yourself do not know the message that you want to put forward to God. This message may be buried so deeply that you are not conscious of it. On the other hand, it could be that you do not trust that God will benevolently and mercifully accept your message. Then there is the silence of the grave that cannot be tolerated for long. Noise, distraction, and diversion are needed.

There is a third kind of stillness—painful and yet healing: silence where stillness is a physician, a therapist; silence before God where stillness is a pearl diver: it dives down to the very depth of our being and returns to the surface with a wound, unsuspected and distressing. Its discovery is hurtful, but God can take it up and heal it, because genuine stillness is nothing less than God himself. He can bring the hidden and unrecognized wounds to our consciousness and cure them. They don't even have to be expressed. We have to let them become conscious, and have to endure them before the loving gaze of God.

This healing gaze of God has a sensitivity so gentle that every therapist would wish to have it. It brings our wounds up into our consciousness, layer by layer, just as they lie within. God will never show a deeper hurt unless its turn has come, because other wounds have to heal first. You don't need to attempt the healing yourself, or to analyze the wounds. No need even to bother about them. They only need to be looked at and gone through patiently in God's presence. His gaze will dissolve them. After all, Jesus Christ has invited us to come to him with burdens of this kind, because he longs to heal us (Matt 11:28). In the dynamics of stillness lies the key to dealing with feelings in contemplative prayer.

Stillness, however, brings about an even greater miracle still. It pulls our attention into a depth where we gaze at God and ourselves. Stillness first makes us experience the biggest obstacle to our oneness with God and ultimately removes it: I am nothing, you are everything; I am a sinner, and you are my Father (Luke 15:22). Ignatius, too, wants to lead us to this miracle at the end of his Exercises (Sp. Exer., 258, 5).

Dear Reader, do you remember times of healing stillness in your life? In what ways did healing come to you?

1 1

The Hundredfold Blessing

L et us return once again to the story of the rich young man (see chapter 6). Peter is eager to know what will happen on that road of emptiness: "Look, we have left everything and followed you" (Mark 10:28). Jesus replies with two promises. For the time after death, he promises eternal life (that is what the rich young man had asked for in the first place). For the present life, Jesus assures the disciples of the blessing—a hundredfold of all they have given up. A "hundredfold blessing": what does that mean?

As long as we endeavor in prayer to think, to plan, to do this, and to do that, our own mental and psychic energies are at work. If, however, we withdraw again and again to our private room, and there learn to focus patiently on the presence of Jesus, energies of a deeper layer come into play. We do not even know how we ought to pray, says Paul; the Holy Spirit is groaning within us in words we cannot pronounce (Rom 8:26). That is the real difference between the level of our own active prayer and the plane of contemplative prayer where God himself is at work. How, concretely, do we reach this second level?

Genuine simplicity will orient our lives toward God. It will bring order into our relationship with ourselves as well as into our relationship with our fellow beings and with the world. Let us now look more closely at just four effects of contemplative prayer.

The first effect is seen in our relationship with God. Communication with God will turn from verbal and mental exchange, and from intimate conversation with him, to the level of wordless and directionless oneness with him. As a result of this, our former spiritual "treasures" like thoughts, feelings, images, and other mental activities will no longer stand between us the creatures and our Creator. In this way, our relationship with God is essentially internalized. It is lifted from the level of conversation and prayerful dialogue to the level of being. Out of this deeper union, and from persevering in it, arises a much more intimate love of God. People who, after many years of mental meditation and other forms of prayer, have found their way to contemplation bear testimony to this.

A second effect of contemplative prayer is that a person will come to a much deeper relationship with him- or herself. We are now much more capable of being *with ourselves*. Once we no longer try to stay with our own thoughts, but instead stay with our deeper selves, our insights arise, not from our rational or psychic level, but from the very depth of our being; that is, from the indwelling God himself. In contemplative prayer, you will discover this quickly. Good ideas come from deeper regions, where thoughts are generally clearer. They hit upon the essentials and do it more simply. Those familiar with Ignatian spirituality will immediately be reminded of the "first election." Grace makes us simpler and more transparent. We begin to acquire clearer perceptions of ourselves and the way ahead of us. Insecurities and anxieties are reduced. We sense that we are in the right place and know now more existentially where our true home is. If Jesus calls this the hundredfold grace, it is no exaggeration.

The experience of the contemplative person is that he or she does nothing. Everything happens all by itself. It is happening through you, but you sense that you are only a tool in the hands of God. This realization may occur even before the practice of contemplative prayer, but it will grow stronger now. An unbelievable freedom arises from finding that you do not carry out activities yourself, but God does. You feel liberated from all worries about your progress and are freed from concern about the results of your endeavors. Out of your center you can trust that "this is the hand of God," because you experience it constantly.

Consider resolutions made, for example, at the conclusion of a retreat. In your former way of "active" praying, you made resolutions and struggled hard to keep them. But in the contemplative phase, resolutions lose their importance. As soon as you learn to spend more time in stillness, you will be happy to discover that everything works out by itself.

All of us are burdened with inordinate inclinations that frequently disturb our lives (Sp. Exer., 1, 4). These may be dissatisfaction, insecurity, fears, depression, sadness, feelings of inferiority, and similar inclinations, almost all of them a result of past experiences. All too often we are not even conscious of them, but if they cause serious disturbance in our daily life, we consult a therapist. Very few people are free of these negative tendencies and the stress they cause. On the level of active prayer or in the phase of "making," in which mental considerations and resolutions still play a role, we try to change our habits. But modifying behavior only helps somewhat, because our inclinations have deeper roots than any habits that we may be able to change by working at them.

It is amazing to see the purifying effect of perfect stillness in the presence of God upon these unconscious tendencies. Perseverance in stillness will allow inclinations to surface, and they will do so in a natural order, layer by layer. As I said in the last chapter, I know no better therapist than stillness. And as I also said, we do not have to work at it: we keep looking at our inclinations, return to our center, and slowly they are dissolved. Stillness is at work in the depths of our being. I find this easier—a hundred times easier—than all the attempts to change myself.

When you expose yourself in prayer, in total emptiness, to the gaze of God, you will discover that in due time, through this same stillness, peace and equanimity enter your daily life. In due course, your growing happiness, even after the time of prayer, is like a melody that keeps playing in the background. Life becomes simple and, in the end, there remains only love. A peaceful energy arises, something you likely have not known earlier. In the midst of the storms of external life, you have only to return to this stillness and at once your deeper center—God's presence—begins to have its effect. You cannot make it yourself. It is purely and only God's work: the fulfillment of Jesus' promise to bless emptiness with a hundredfold gift.

A third effect of contemplation shows itself in our dealings with our neighbor. We can have contact with others only at that depth which we have reached in ourselves first, and at which we continue to exist. In dealing with others, we discover that we communicate on the very same plane on which we ourselves live. No one can touch another person on a deeper level than that on which he has first found access to himself. Thus, as long as we move on the level of doing, organizing, and talking, we will hardly be able to affect others more deeply or be able to help them. Through contemplation, reverence grows in our relationships with our neighbors. On the one hand we will recognize more clearly the inordinate tendencies in our neighbor, along with his or her darkness; on the other hand we will nevertheless find growing respect for the person's dignity. Is not our time of being lost in silent presence before Jesus a hundredfold better preparation for dealing with other people than any other "method"?

Efficacy will shift from doing to radiance. The effect of radiance is, of course, not an exclusive privilege of the contemplative way. But only in the contemplative realm will its effect be felt clearly. Activities, I feel, are given too much importance in most undertakings, and even more so, unfortunately, in pastoral ministry.

Jesus, too, was active. But people were eager to come near him simply because of his radiance: a great power went out of him, they would say. Jesus healed through his presence. For him healing and proclaiming the Gospel belonged together. When he said to his disciples, "Proclaim the good news," he told them at the same time to go and heal (Matt 10:7, 8). It is not that Jesus is ordering us to work miracles, but that he wants us to be rooted in him to such a degree that merely by dealing with us, people will be made well. In contemplation, efficacy will migrate from doing to radiating. Let us remember our saints: their very existence was a source of healing. Could it not be a blessing, in all our pastoral and social activities, to shift the center of gravity from doing to radiance?

A fourth of the hundredfold effects of contemplation—resting in the still center with our gaze on the presence of Jesus Christ—may also be seen in our relationship with the world. In active prayer, our purpose is to acquire a certain measure of independence from the world. As I mentioned earlier, Ignatius calls this "indifference" (Sp. Exer., 23, 5); that is, we no longer desire health over sickness, a long life over a short one. Such a state is desirable, of course, and one can work to achieve it. But, don't forget that the impulse toward preservation, health, and life is such an essential drive in humanity that it cannot be wiped out by willpower. However, through the process of constant, alert resting at the ground of our being, independence from our desires may be given to us as a gift.

Grace of this kind is a hundredfold blessing. Happy or unhappy, fortunate or unfortunate, in the contemplative phase of prayer you will be, as it were, untouched by the waves of destiny. Initially this will happen only in prayer. If, however, you can make it a habit to withdraw to your private room regularly, you will soon find that the seemingly unsolvable problems pressing on you from the outside world will lose their impact on you. As you progress on the contemplative way, your "untouchability"—or rather immunity—from the storms of

life will steadily extend beyond prayer to the rest of
daily life.

⚬⚬⚬

*Dear Reader, have you ever come across a person
whose radiance seemed to come from a "Sun" hidden
deep inside? How did your encounter with that person affect you?*

12

A Fleeting Glance
at Mysticism

In the course of life, a person will pass through
several stages in his or her relationship to God.
This is mirrored most clearly in changes in the
person's prayer life. The individual stages of prayer
evolve slowly. They don't change from one day to
the other, just as you do not become an adult one
day after puberty ends. Long before a new level of
prayer really begins, certain elements may emerge.
Often, a person's prayer may encompass qualities
touching two or three levels at once.

The literature on prayer divides it into two
types: *active prayer* and *passive prayer*. Active

prayer includes all the prayers in which the praying person is active. Active prayer has four stages, as described in my book *Lernen wir beten* (2nd ed., Würzburg: Echter, 2000). Passive prayer, on the other hand, is prayer in which God is the active one; here the person is merely and simply open, and passively receives the grace of prayer. This prayer has four stages, too, and we shall list them here as well.

Every level of prayer also brings along with it a process of purification suited to the stage—active purification, in which a person endeavors to bring about change, or passive purification, in which God himself slowly wipes out the imperfections still clinging to the person.

Active Prayer

With the very first word that a child begins to utter, the opportunity to address God in words also arises. We call this *oral prayer*. The child learns the Our Father, the Hail Mary, and other prayers; repeats them word by word; and soon knows them by heart. These stir up feelings toward God and make it possible for the child to experience its first conscious contact with him. Of course, it is not only children who find their access to God through oral prayer. All religious people address God. By oral prayer, we simply mean that the emphasis is still on the words, and not yet on the mental and emotional planes.

As the infant grows, reason more and more serves as a source of awakening. As children or teenagers, we begin to ask questions about our surroundings, the problems of our life, our relationships, and—finally—the big question about the meaning of life. Reason plays an important role now. Consequently, teenagers will apply their intellect while turning to God, by asking questions, reflecting, and discerning. The result of these mental activities will be decisions. Since the intellect dominates prayer at this level, we call it *mental prayer*. Anyone familiar with the Ignatian Exercises will recognize in this type of prayer the Reflections of the First Week. Purification during this phase of prayer comes through the insight of reason.

Along with reason, the emotional element now enters in. During puberty and afterward, the world of feelings awakens more and more. The young boy or girl will also turn to God with all this: changing passions, mood swings, resistance, devotion, and gratitude—a big basketful of feelings and emotions. And all of this will somehow also find its way into prayer. The life of Jesus is the best resource for this prayer. Using the traditional Latin concept, we call it *affective prayer*.

When you pray like this, you first choose a Gospel text, read it, and let it act upon you. Then the really personal part follows: based on the passage, you confront your life and actions with the life of Jesus. What message does Jesus' life, as seen in this text, have for you? How and with whom can you identify in this reading? Thus, a kind of bridge will grow between the events of the life of Jesus and the events of your own. You become aware of which aspects of life and actions do not correspond to the Gospel, and make up your mind to change that. Finally, you may turn to Jesus personally, or to the Father, and share with him your discoveries and plans.

Meditations of this kind may allow you to develop a very intimate relationship with Jesus and God the Father. This phase of prayer may go beyond the years of puberty and may lead to intimacy in one's spiritual life. Such meditations on the life of Jesus may lead into a life of discipleship for someone who goes deep enough. Purification in this phase of prayer does not remain merely rational, but also permeates the psyche. Unconscious and unsolved burdens will be actively worked upon. People will notice that this is a person with a deep spiritual life: his or her example will radiate outward.

As a person grows in calmness and inner simplicity, such an individual's prayer life too will become increasingly simpler. A quiet sense of wonder will slowly be added to words, thoughts, and devotional feelings. The person may then take up a short text, perhaps just a sentence from a psalm that touches him or her deeply, and will go on repeating it for days and weeks on end. Inside, a loving surrender to God begins to blossom. This happens most often after the storms of life have slowly given way to greater calmness. Words, thoughts, and emotions lose a lot of their intensity, although they may not, however, vanish all together. Purification is quieter. The simple relationship with God takes on more weight. It is *simple prayer*, and it is indeed a simplified version of affective prayer.

In the Exercises, Ignatius leads us to affective and simple prayer by meditation on the life of Jesus.

Passive Prayer, or Mysticism

Simple prayer is the last kind of active prayer, prayer we can practice by ourselves (assisted, of course, by grace). What follows is then no longer our doing. We become passive recipients. God draws our attention to himself. We experience a growing desire to see God—not merely his creation anymore, but God himself. More and more we sense that longing for the face of God. But initially the vision is not given. What can one do then? We cannot conjure up the vision of God by our own activity. But paradoxically, we will nonetheless be able to do one thing: in prayer, we can still turn our attention *away from* texts, thoughts, images, and feelings, *away from* our expectations and aspirations—that is, from the content of prayer—and *turn directly to* the face of

God, to Jesus Christ, to his name, or to the person of the Father.

The longing for the contemplative vision is already there, but the grace of contemplation—that is, *contemplatio infusa*—may still be missing. I call even this longing contemplative prayer. It is how contemplative prayer begins—as a transition between the four levels of active prayer and the contemplative state proper, the steps of which we shall discuss shortly. We are tied to active prayer because it is still our doing. Yet we are bound to the passive form of prayer by the fact that our activity is now restricted to the mere gazing on God, independent of whether or not we have been granted the experience or grace of vision.

Contemplative prayer is what St. Ignatius considers the Third Method of Praying, coming after forms of active prayer (Sp. Exer., 258).

Once God himself begins to lead a person's prayer by grace, the way is known as "mysticism." There are another four stages on the mystical way, a detailed study of which would go beyond the purpose of this book. But we can give a simplified account of them here for the purpose of orientation and to complete our overview. St. Teresa of Avila, whose teachings caused her to be named a doctor of the church, describes the four stages in her book *Interior Castle*.

The first stage is the *prayer of recollection*. God draws in your will so much that you no longer have distractions in prayer. You are fascinated by the presence of God to such a degree that you rest in wonder before him for a long time, without interruption. You don't "pray" as such, but are simply aware of God's presence. Meditating on texts becomes a hindrance at this point, if not earlier. Prayer no longer deals with texts, because your attention is now focused more directly and exclusively on God (as put by St. John of the Cross, in *Ascent to Mount Carmel*). Only now can we begin to talk of contemplation in the proper sense.

Thoughts may still skate, as it were, around the edges of our awareness. But we are no longer preoccupied with them, remaining steadily attentive to God. Now the passive purification of our senses begins. St. John of the Cross calls this the "dark night of the senses." God purifies darkness that has lingered, deep down, in spite of the long spiritual journey undergone before. Purification is in the region of the psyche, but the manner is passive. We have touched on this in chapter 10 on stillness. On this level of prayer, one's radiance is remarkably strong. Many people do not attain the prayer of recollection.

The second stage of mysticism is *simple union*. God takes possession of consciousness to such an extent that a person has no more thoughts. While the grace of prayer and of freedom from thoughts lasts, his or her attention is focused on the presence of Jesus Christ or the Father. The experience of God is so intense that even a long time after the experience, you have no doubt that it was God you saw!

The great conversions and extraordinary calls, like those of Paul or of the apostle Matthew (Sp. Exer., 175), or the vision of Ignatius on the river Cardoner, belong to this stage. The night of the senses continues. People gifted with this grace possess not only radiance, but also a healing presence whereby they exert great influence on all they encounter. Many saints have been led to this stage, at least toward the end of their lives.

The third stage is *ecstatic union*. Here God also takes possession of the senses; the person has no contact with the surrounding world while the union lasts. Upon occasion, or even repeatedly, he or she may experience ecstasy: the saints frequently report visions of the humanity of Jesus Christ. In ecstasy, a person is taken through the night of the spirit: a very painful and radical purification. He can hardly tolerate the Light of God striking him and—seemingly a contradiction—feels forsaken by God until grace prepares him for this inconceivable Light of God. It may come to a mystical betrothal: for a moment, God grants the person the experience of eternal life. This, of course, transcends our normal power of human imagination. The stage of mystical marriage might also be reached, indicating that the union with God is unceasing and indissoluble. Understandably, this state is much rarer than simple union.

The fourth stage of mysticism is *transforming union*. God takes possession of the whole person. Totally permeated by God, he or she is separated from eternal life only by a single last step. To outward observance, such a person is a perfectly normal human being devoid of ecstasies or extraordinary phenomena. This individual moves around freely in the world and in most cases is very active. But in the person's innermost being, he or she tastes unceasing oneness with God. The exceptional thing is that the person radiates only love and light. People like this—literally "full of grace"—exert an extraordinary influence upon many nations and many generations. Think of the great saints: Paul, Augustine, Benedict, Francis of Assisi, Ignatius, Teresa of Avila, and Thérèse of Lisieux, to name a few. They are like Christ on earth.

We shouldn't wrack our brains over these stages of prayer or be anxious to indulge in debates about them. That would contribute neither to an understanding of them nor to a more profound relationship with God. We will never understand them anyway. It is quite enough to cultivate in ourselves a deep reverence and respect for the mighty works of God and to look to our future with great hope and joy.

I have wanted only to direct our considerations and to show which dimensions tend to open up when God himself guides us by his hand. If my presentation helps to stir in you the desire for the face of God in Christ Jesus, or to quicken your surrender and deepen your sense of service to him, I will have achieved my goal, and this book will have served its purpose.

Dear Reader, can you imagine that one day God may grant you graces that altogether transcend the realm of mere human endeavor? Have you had a taste of this kind of grace already?

13

An Example

We have been reflecting on the contemplative way from different perspectives. Still missing is an illustration. What is contemplative prayer all about? We shall take our example from Ignatius. As I said, he calls contemplative prayer the Third Method of Praying. In the Spiritual Exercises it is the last of the methods of prayer (Sp. Exer., 258–60).*

Just as he does for the other two methods of prayer, Ignatius provides a framework: an opening and a concluding conversation with God (Sp. Exer., 239–40; 257). There follows a recommended body posture; for this prayer, he suggests an attitude of

---

* More about the meaning of this way to pray may be found in my article "Die kontemplative Phase der ignatianischen Exerzitien," in *Spiritualität im Wandel*, ed. Andreas Schoenfeld (Wurzburg: Echter Verlag, 2002), 344–63.

deep recollection, sitting or kneeling. The retreatant may keep his or her eyes closed or focus them on a particular point (Sp. Exer., 252, 1).

Attention to breathing is important during this prayer: we should pronounce every word with one breath, and Ignatius emphasizes that we should not use more than one word between two breaths. In contemplative prayer, attention to breathing almost always plays an important role.

In all earlier reflections and meditations, Ignatius has provided accompanying tasks—to look out for meanings, comparisons, tastes, or consolations. Now, however, he limits prayer to looking (gazing). To look at what? Initially, we may focus on the word we speak. Think of the Jesus Prayer, in which the word would be the name of Jesus. But here, attention is not to be given only to a word's meaning. We are to *look at the person himself*, the person whose name we have used. It is a matter of a relationship with God, and Ignatius emphasizes the need to attend to that relationship: we reflect on our own lowliness, or on the difference between the greatness of God, to whom the prayer is being addressed, and our own littleness (Sp. Exer., 258, 5).

Thus, we may say that this prayer consists exclusively in looking (gazing); namely, in looking at God and our relationship with God. This prayer has an eminent place in the Exercises for three reasons: First, it belongs essentially to the core of the Exercises. Ignatius is very clear that the Spiritual

Exercises are not complete unless we have practiced this prayer.* Second, Ignatius introduces here an essentially new prayer that, deviating from all earlier methods of praying, is fully centered on looking. Third, it is the last kind of prayer, and the last exercise with which Ignatius sends the retreatant back into life. With this kind of prayer we have reached the place to which Ignatius planned to take us. If during the time of his retreat, we sensed at least a gentle breath of contemplative prayer and if, through that, a desire for the face of God was kindled, then we are not likely ever to forget this new way of praying.

Ignatius did not write long treatises on contemplation; that was never his style. But his resolution and way of leading to contemplative prayer is presented in the book of Exercises briefly and pointedly. We may ask why Ignatius did not write more extensively about contemplative prayer. The simplest answer might be that it is hard to set down in

* At the beginning of the Spiritual Exercises (4), Ignatius explains the structure and duration of the four parts and includes the Three Methods of Praying with the Fourth Part, making clear that these are intrinsic to the Exercises. The decisive element of the four parts is not the matter of the meditation, but whether or not the aim of each has been achieved (the "attaining what is sought"). That really means that the Exercises are not complete unless the "looking at God" of the Third Method of Praying has been genuinely experienced. (They may not in fact be completed unless the retreatant's spiritual level permits it [18], but in that case the aim is not achieved even if the retreat lasted its full thirty days.)

black and white what happens without thoughts and only by looking. Ignatius was never a man of many words, but he was a great mystic and familiar with the paths of souls. It might well have dawned on him that the time would come when many men and women would be hungering for the contemplative way. That is why he writes into the Spiritual Exercises, concisely and unmistakably, just enough so that people of his time would not feel overburdened or people of future generations find insufficient direction. Today few things are more urgently needed than the rediscovery of the contemplative way. Is it not wonderful that we are able to give a corresponding answer out of the treasure trove of our own venerable Jesuit tradition?

Dear Reader, can you imagine that in the course of time your meditations may simplify into a silent gaze at our Creator and Redeemer? If so, what further steps might you consider undertaking?

A Little Flower

I first heard the expression "signs of the time" during the period of the Second Vatican Council. Things began to move in the church then, and it was high time to change structures. That caused anxieties in many people. The life of the church is guided by God, and they felt that they were being asked to deviate from the way God had always shown and to search for new ways. That was unsettling and a source of anxiety. The representatives of the *aggiornamento*, the renewal, were quick to answer that it was really God himself who has given us signs that he wants to lead the church to new ways, that during the decades before the council we were too slow to recognize these signs. "Search for the signs of the time" was the big slogan. For many people, this expression awakened hope and made them feel that we are a living church.

Today the church is in crisis, just as in the years before the council. It hurts to say it, but the monasteries, convents, and houses of religious congregations, once the foundation of the church—are not most of them now retirement homes? Those religious who still do have strength are overworked, often at the cost of prayer. Priests in pastoral ministry are put in charge of more and more parishes. Isn't it obvious that they are busier with organizational matters than with the spiritual renewal of believers? With a steady decline in attendance, churches are becoming increasingly empty. Many—not all, thanks be to God—fail to respond adequately to real needs.

Could it be, perhaps, that there is too much doing and too much talking? Would it not be better if every parish community were given an opportunity to learn the way of contemplative prayer that so many search for? And would it not be true to Ignatius's purpose to have leaders trained to guide others competently through a contemplative retreat? Isn't it true that the renewal of the church has always started with a renewal from within? And could it not be, therefore, that the most urgent and pressing "sign of the times" is God's call to contemplative prayer?

Many Catholics leave the church to join breakaway Christian sects, or even other religions, because they don't find the contemplative way in the church. That was not the case forty or fifty years ago, but even then Karl Rahner had clearly recognized this tendency: he said that the Christian of the future would either be a mystic or else not a Christian at all. That statement is quoted frequently, proving that this is a truth most people today understand. The fact that the vast majority of Christians today are *not* mystics points back to our prayer life. Wouldn't the proper reaction to all this be to consider seriously contemplative prayer? No doubt, a hunger for the contemplative way is felt in our times. Can we begin to see this as a powerful "sign of the times" through which God wants to "quicken a new springtime in the Church"?

The spiritual man or woman of today feels a remarkable desire for contemplative prayer. He or she is looking—as never before in human history— for the simplicity and calm of the contemplative way. *Rush* is the word that increasingly typifies our time; all the more, then, do we need the quietness of mere sitting, looking, gazing. The more complex the world gets, the more we need contemplative simplicity. The more the world literally besieges us with the shallow empty words of propaganda and advertisement, the more we need the wordless, noiseless space of stillness in order to get closer to our true nature. The more our several years of study, the media, electronics, and all of modern life challenge us to quick thinking, the more we need to balance the rush with a contemplative outlook. The more the nations of the world indulge in wars and our families live in tension and strife, the more we require the harmony and peace of the contemplative way.

The need for the contemplative way is great. Our response, that of all those concerned, may be seen as a tiny little flower. In times of crisis we are in danger of hammering out big plans and discussing what and how to change. I believe there is a better strategy. It is not we who need to invent new ways. God shows them to us. We only need to discover where new life is to be found. God is at work making new life a sign of the times.

The new life begins like the little flower. Just watch closely how it grows: at first you hardly notice how the tip of the blade, bit by bit, slowly creeps out of the soil, but it doesn't take long till the flower is in full bloom—all by itself! We only have to keep our eyes wide open and observe closely where new life is in the making. The new little flower wants to grow. And we, for our part, have to protect it, foster its growth, and take care to see that enough sun and rain reach it and that it isn't damaged. These are the hopes of a new future. Long ago Jesus Christ spoke about the mustard seed and reminded us to pay attention to the little flowers of the future (Matt 13:31).

In the midst of the rush of this world, countless people are searching for simple prayer and a peaceful life. For me that is a striking sign of the times, a little flower that we need to guard, to water, and to move into the sun. It is a little flame, meant to become a mighty fire. We should recognize the call of God because it is Jesus Christ who, through this sign of the times, wants to lead us on the way to the Father from faith to mere looking or gazing.

Dear Reader, at the present moment of history, what signs of the times do you observe? What are those

tiny unpretentious flowers that have a great future because God is behind them? Where among these signs would you place the way of contemplation?

15

Let Us Begin

Dear Reader, I have broadly outlined the contemplative way for you. Perhaps it roused something within you, and you feel a desire to walk along that way yourself. I would like to describe a few beginning steps that may help you.

A Retreat as a Beginning

Perhaps you have attended retreats more than once or have been meditating on the life of Jesus in the Gospels. That is the ideal preparation for the grace of contemplation. In and through contact with the Gospel, Sacred Scripture, and the life of Jesus, God frequently confers contemplative graces. If you have sensed that your reflections were becoming simplified, bringing about more quietness, or awakening the desire merely to look at God himself, you know that the grace of contemplation has begun to work in you. That is a call from God urging a response, which could well mean learning a contemplative way of praying.

A learning process is needed for us to handle the flood of distractions that keep us from merely looking at God. Then, too, feelings like dryness or dullness may arise to distract us. As we are initiated into contemplative prayer, our attention is being trained in how to handle these distractions. We do not have to cease our familiar ways of praying, but acquiring the way of contemplative prayer will enable the focal point of prayer to be shifted—spontaneously and at the right moment—to where the Spirit wants to lead us.

To learn more about contemplative prayer, I recommend my book *Contemplative Retreat* (Longwood, FL: Xulon Press, 2003). Permit me, please, to do a little personal sharing here about this book. After twenty-five years of giving contemplative retreats, I wanted to publish my experiences in order to give many more people access to them. I recorded more than 2,000 interviews, or "dialogues," with my retreatants. With that material I then began to work on a typical model of a retreat. I reflected on the kinds of themes or questions that surfaced and how often and at what points in the retreat process I had to respond. I selected about 200 of the recorded interviews to become the core of my book and divided them into ten days, just as my retreats at that time lasted a full ten days. To the interviews I added ten talks I used to give, together with the necessary instructions for each day. The book thus became a guide, a handbook for making a retreat all by oneself, either in days of perfect stillness or as a retreat in daily life, spread over weeks or months. Even apart from making this retreat, you may profit by reading one or more of the dialogues before or after the time you spend in contemplative prayer; in this way it may become a companion to your daily prayer. Again, if you make your retreat with the help of the book, it will guide you step-by-step through the ten days. But for those with still deeper interest, I would recommend that you try to attend a contemplative retreat.

Exercises in Relationship

A good introduction to the contemplative way of life may be found in the following four exercises, even before you buy a book such as mine or embark on a retreat. These exercises are based on the parallels between our relationship with God and relationships with other people. If you find it hard to let people come close to you and to accept them, it will be nearly impossible to experience the presence of God. If you are unable to listen to your neighbor, you will not be able to endure the attentive stillness face to face with God.

    1. You are part of a group of people engaged in a debate. The discussion is heating up more

and more. Do not pay attention to the main topic of the discussion, and refrain from expressing what you had in mind as an important contribution to be made. Instead, just listen to the person who is most engaged in the discussion. All you are to do is to listen to him or her. You are doing this simply to understand the other person from the inside. You try to sense what that person is going through at that moment. Finally, drop your remaining intention to express your opinion when the debate is over.

2. You are in a debate again, similar to the first example, but now the heat is more intense. You are in the thick of it, with you and your partner in close conversation. Try to do exactly what you did in the first exercise—just listen, up to the very end of the discussion, and at the end say only, "I think I have understood what you said," or, "I want to allow what you've said to act on me even more." This is not easy, but it is a very good way to learn "looking" and awareness in daily life.

3. You are in conversation again. It is interesting and very lively. You are deeply involved and want to express something important. Try to drop the idea and switch over to mere listening. Do this even when you feel strongly that your contribution would be so important that it would lead the discussion to its end-

point. Try to show interest in nothing else but the opinion of your partner, and forget about the message that you thought you had to throw in. In contemplative prayer you have to listen to God. Your own thoughts are of little use here.

4. You feel stress in an irritating situation at home or at work. Try to look at the pressure without wanting to change it. Just be aware of it, and continue in this awareness until the pressure starts alleviating itself and then gets dissolved.

Take, Lord, and receive all my liberty, my memory, my understanding, and all my will—all that I have and possess. You, Lord, have given all that to me. I now give it back to you, O Lord. All of it is yours. Dispose of it according to your will. Give me your love and your grace, for that is enough for me. (Sp. Exer., 234)

About the Author

Franz Jalics, SJ, was born in 1927 in Budapest, Hungary, and grew up on his father's estate, setting out to become a professional soldier as his father wished. But at the end of World War II, he spent time in Germany as a refugee and returned to Hungary in 1946, where he completed high school and entered the Jesuit Order. In the early 1950s, he began studies in literature and languages in Pullach, near Munich, Germany. In 1954, he earned his degree in philosophy at Leuven-Eegenhoven, Belgium, after which he spent two years as an educator in southern Belgium, in a Jesuit high school at Mons. In 1956, the Society of Jesus sent him to Chile, and a year later to Argentina, where he remained for the next twenty years. He studied theology and was ordained a priest in 1959.

Father Jalics taught dogmatics and fundamental theology at the Jesuit San Miguel University. In 1963, he also became the students' spiritual director and began to give retreats. He earned his PhD in theology in 1966.

At the beginning of the 1970s, Father Jalics and two fellow Jesuits went to live in the slums to share their life with the poor. In 1976, an ultraconservative group kidnapped him and imprisoned him in an undisclosed location. For five months he was their captive, blindfolded and tied hand and foot. He was released surreptitiously and without explanation. He left Argentina late in 1977 and spent a year in the United States and Canada. Since 1978, he has lived in Germany, devoting himself to leading retreats, and since 1984, he has had his own retreat house in Gries, Wilhelmsthal, Germany.

His early books include *El encuentro con Dios* (1970), *Cambios en la fe* (1972), *Aprendiendo a orar* (1973), and *Aprendiendo a compartir la fe* (1978). His practical introduction to contemplation has been published in German (Echter Verlag, 1994), in English (*Contemplative Retreat,* Xulon Press, 2003), and in eight other languages.

ILLUMINATIONBOOKS

Other Books in the Series

Finding God Today
E. Springs Steele

Hail Mary and Rhythmic Breathing
Richard Galentino

The Eucharist
Joseph M. Champlin

Gently Grieving
Constance M. Mucha

Devotions for Caregivers
Marilyn Driscoll

Carrying the Cross with Christ
Rev. Joseph T. Sullivan

Be a Blessing
Elizabeth M. Nagel

The Art of Affirmation
Robert Furey

Jesus' Love Stories
John F. Loya & Joseph A. Loya

Compassionate Awareness
Adolfo Quezada

Finding a Grace-Filled Life
Rick Mathis

Mystical Prayer Is for (*Almost*) Everyone
Ernest J. Fiedler

Life, Death, and Christian Hope
Daneen Georgy Warner

Radical Love
Adolfo Quezada

The Image of God
Mark Plaiss

Meditations for Eucharistic Adoration
Bonnie Taylor Barry